Star Baby

For Kate Hammer and Audrey
I.W.

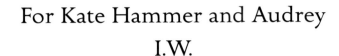

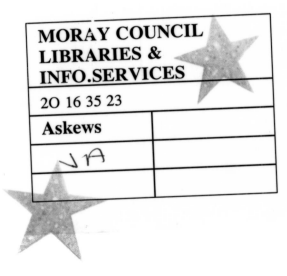
ORCHARD BOOKS
96 Leonard Street, London EC2A 4XD
Hachette Children's Books
Level 17/207 Kent Street, Sydney, NSW 2000
First published in Great Britain in 2005
ISBN 1 84362 839 2
Text © Ian Whybrow 2005
Illustrations © Jason Cockcroft 2005
The rights of Ian Whybrow to be identified as the author and Jason Cockcroft to
be identified as the illustrator of this work have been asserted by them
in accordance with the Copyright, Designs and Patents Act, 1988.
A CIP catalogue record for this book is available from the British Library.
1 3 5 7 9 10 8 6 4 2
Printed in Singapore

Star Baby

Ian Whybrow

Illustrated by Jason Cockcroft

ORCHARD BOOKS

Stars are like babies,

The moon's little babies.

Bright little babies,

Just like mine.

Every star baby

Knows how to please us.

Every one that sees us

Loves to shine shine shine.

The sheep has got a baby,

A nice woolly baby.

The sheep's little baby

Doesn't run far.

The sheep's little baby

Knows how to please her -

When he sees her

The lamb says baaaa.

The horse has got a baby,

A leggy little baby.

This leggy baby

Knows what to say.

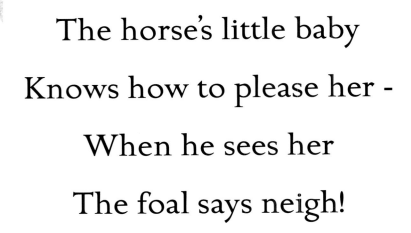

The horse's little baby

Knows how to please her -

When he sees her

The foal says neigh!

The cow has got a baby,

A soft little baby.

The cow's little baby

Knows what to do.

The cow's little baby

Knows how to please her -

When he sees her

The calf says moo.

The hen has got babies,

Snug little babies.

Six little babies

Settle down to sleep.

The hen's little babies

Know how to please her -

Every chick that sees her

Says cheep cheep cheep.

I've got a baby,

The best little baby.

You're my baby

This little while.

My little baby

Knows how to please me -

First you squeeze me

And then you smile.

The world is full of babies,
Beautiful babies.
The world feels better
Where babies are.

Every little baby
Knows how to please us -
Every one that sees us
Shines like a star.